W9-ANN-354

COPING WITH . . .
PLASTIC TRASH

COPING WITH . . .
PLASTIC TRASH

Jamie Daniel • Veronica Bonar
Illustrated by Tony Kenyon

Gareth Stevens Publishing
MILWAUKEE

For a free color catalog describing Gareth Stevens' list of high-quality books, call 1-800-341-3569 (USA) or 1-800-461-9120 (Canada).

Library of Congress Cataloging-in-Publication Data

Daniel, Jamie.
    Coping with— plastic trash/adapted from Veronica Bonar's Plastic rubbish! by Jamie Daniel; illustrated by Tony Kenyon. — North American ed.
        p. cm. — (Trash busters)
    Includes bibliographical references and index.
    ISBN 0-8368-1060-0
    1. Plastic scrap—Juvenile literature. 2. Refuse and refuse disposal—Juvenile literature. [1. Plastic—recycling. 2. Refuse and refuse disposal. 3. Recycling (Waste)] I. Kenyon, Tony, ill. II. Bonar, Veronica. Plastic rubbish! III. Title. IV. Series: Daniel, Jamie. Trash busters.
TD798.D364   1994
363.72'82--dc20   93-37687

This North American edition first published in 1994 by
Gareth Stevens Publishing
1555 North RiverCenter Drive, Suite 201
Milwaukee, WI 53212, USA

This edition © 1994 by Zoë Books Limited. First produced as *PLASTIC RUBBISH!*, © 1992 by Zoë Books Limited, original text © 1992 by Veronica Bonar. Additional end matter © 1994 by Gareth Stevens, Inc. Published in the USA by arrangement with Zoë Books Limited, Winchester, England. Published in Canada by arrangement with Heinemann Educational Books Ltd., Oxford, England.

Series editor: Patricia Lantier-Sampon
Cover design: Karen Knutson

Picture Credits:
The Environmental Picture Library p. 12 (Stan Gamester); Robert Harding Picture Library pp. 7, 10, 26; Courtesy of ICI p. 8; Science Photo Library p. 14 (Dr. Morley Read), p. 19 (Hank Morgan), pp. 21, 22 (James Holmes/Zedcor), p. 25 (Peter Ryan); Zefa p. 17.

Printed in the USA

1 2 3 4 5 6 7 8 9 99 98 97 96 95 94

At this time, Gareth Stevens, Inc., does not use 100 percent recycled paper, although the paper used in our books does contain about 30 percent recycled fiber. This decision was made after a careful study of current recycling procedures revealed their dubious environmental benefits. We will continue to explore recycling options.

TABLE OF CONTENTS

Words that appear in the glossary are printed in **boldface** type the first time they occur in the text.

PLASTIC EVERYWHERE YOU LOOK!

Plastic is tough, lightweight, and does not rust or fall apart. Many everyday items, such as toys, telephones, and radios, are made of plastic. So are lots of things in the kitchen, from bowls to spoons to milk cartons to plastic bags. Some car parts are made of plastic, and food and drinks are often sold in plastic containers.

Plastics do not all look or act alike. Some are soft and spongy, such as the plastic used in foam pillows. Others are hard and clear and act like glass. Some plastics can crack easily, while others, such as those used to make beach balls, are flexible. And plastics can be any color, or they can be clear.

← Many beach toys are made of plastic.

HOW PLASTIC IS MADE

⬆ This plastic reel was formed in a **mold**.

People first discovered how to make plastic about 150 years ago. But the types of plastics we use today are only about sixty years old. Most plastics are made from **oil**, and a few are made from **coal**. Making goods out of plastic is quicker and less expensive than making them out of metal or wood. Two main types of plastic are used for most plastic products today.

We use **thermoplastics** more than any other kind of plastic. Hot thermoplastic can be molded into almost any shape. After it cools, thermoplastic stays hard and keeps its shape. But it can melt again if it gets hot.

Thermosets are plastics that are squeezed into shape under high **pressure**. Objects made this way will not melt if they get hot. Electric plugs are made of thermoset plastics.

9

PLASTIC PACKAGING

Many of the items we buy every day come in plastic packages. Plastic packaging is inexpensive and lightweight, and it can also help keep food fresh longer.

⬆ This fruit is wrapped in plastic to make shopping easier and to keep the fruit fresh.

Most plastic packaging is only used for a short time. Many people throw the plastic wrap away as soon as they open a package. In addition, many plastic frozen dinner containers are made to be used only once and then tossed into the garbage.

PLASTIC TRASH

⬆ Plastic trash carried by the wind often gets caught in trees and bushes.

About 25 percent of our trash is plastic. Everyone should separate certain plastics from the rest of their trash for recycling. If we do not recycle plastics, they are taken to **landfills** along with other garbage and buried underground.

Most plastic trash is not **biodegradable** like food, wood, or paper; it does not **decompose**. Plastic items can lie buried for hundreds of years. Many times, plastic blows away in the wind before it can be buried in landfills.

PLASTIC LITTER

Plastic **litter** is often thrown off ships into our lakes and seas. This plastic does not decay, and it eventually washes up on beaches around the world. Plastic objects floating in the water can kill fish and other animals. Seals and dolphins can strangle in old plastic fishing nets. Fish swallow entire pieces of plastic.

⬆ This plastic litter washed up on the beach after being dumped into the sea.

Plastic litter on the ground is dangerous, too. Plastic bags and sheets of plastic can trap and **suffocate** birds and other animals. Plastic can also be dangerous to children. Plastic bags usually carry a warning that children can suffocate if allowed to play with the bags.

PLASTIC THAT BREAKS DOWN

Since most plastic is not biodegradable, it will not decay or break down and disappear into the soil. But scientists have invented a special plastic with an **additive** that at least lets the plastic break down into small pieces.

Some biodegradable plastics break down in the sunlight. Others contain natural substances that break down in soil. But these plastics only break down into small pieces. The pieces still are not fully biodegradable, so they will never completely disappear.

Biodegradable plastics have many uses. Doctors use plastic thread in some operations. The plastic thread slowly breaks down and passes out of the body as waste.

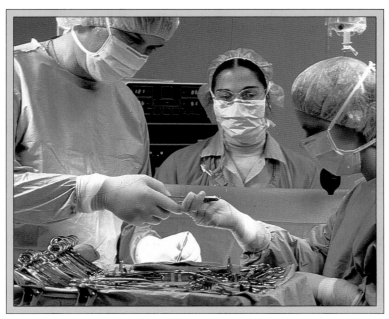

▲ Doctors sometimes use plastic thread in operations.

17

PLASTIC AS FUEL

We are quickly using up the world's natural supply of oil and coal. We use oil and coal as fuel, as well as for making plastics. If we do not slow down and **conserve** these substances, they will become more and more rare and will cost much more in the future.

18

Plastic burns cleanly at high temperatures. It can be burned in an **incinerator**, and it helps other trash burn more quickly. Plastic produces less air **pollution** when burned than other materials. Some countries use burning plastic to produce heat and **electricity**.

▲ Plastic trash is being loaded into an incinerator.

RECYCLING PLASTIC

All thermoplastics can be **recycled**.
From homes and recycling centers, they
can be taken to a factory and melted
down to make new items. Unfortunately,
most plastics are not being recycled.
The factory process is expensive, and
many people would rather just throw
plastics away in their homes than take
the time to sort them for recycling.

⬆ These rolls of plastic sheets are made from recycled plastic.

Some plastics can be melted down and reused more easily than others. For example, new food and drink containers can only be made from one type of recycled plastic. But other items, such as trash bags, coat hangers, and patio furniture, can be made from different plastics mixed together.

RULES FOR RECYCLING

In some countries, people have special containers, or bins, in their homes and businesses for different types of recyclable trash. Plastic trash goes into one of these containers after the plastic has been cleaned.

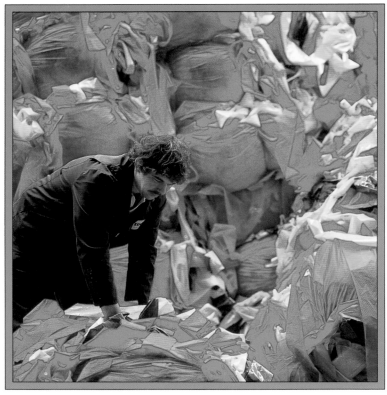

▲ These plastic bags will be recycled into rolls of plastic sheets.

All parts not made of plastic should also be removed from plastic trash before dropping it into the recycling bin. Then the plastic trash can be crushed either at home or at the recycling center so it takes up less space.

PLASTIC BOTTLES

Sometimes people must pay a **deposit** on glass bottles of soda at the time of purchase. The customer gets the deposit back when the empty bottles are returned. The bottles can then be used again. Many plastic drink bottles do not require a deposit because they cannot be **sterilized** and reused like glass.

⬆ These bales of plastic bottles will be recycled into rolls of plastic.

Plastic bottles ready for recycling are flattened into **bales** so they can be easily moved. The recycled plastic will be used to make such products as plastic furniture, gardening pots, or rolls of plastic material.

REUSING PLASTIC

⬆ This colorful kite is made of plastic.

An important way to recycle plastic is to use items more than once. Plastic bags from stores can be used several times to carry groceries and other items. They can also be used as trash bags. Plastic yogurt containers are great for starting plants from seed for your garden.

Plastic containers can be reused several times instead of just throwing them away. Those filled with cottage cheese or margarine are handy for storing leftovers. They are also great to use as freezer containers because they are usually **airtight**. Recycling trash of all kinds will help protect our environment.

GLOSSARY

additive: a substance that has been added to another substance.

airtight: closed so tightly that no air can get in.

bales: large bundles of goods that have been pressed together to take up as little space as possible.

biodegradable: able to be broken down by bacteria.

coal: a natural substance found in the earth that is black in color and used as a fuel. Coal forms from partly decayed plant matter.

conserve: to use resources sparingly so they are not wasted.

decompose: to break down completely and rot, or decay.

deposit: a small amount of extra money paid when something is bought. For example, people usually must pay deposits on returnable glass bottles at the time of purchase. They get the money back if and when they return the bottles.

electricity: a type of energy that can either be found in nature or manufactured by humans. Some countries burn plastic to make electricity.

incinerators: containers for burning waste materials.

landfills: big holes in the ground where trash is dumped and then covered with soil.

litter: the trash people carelessly throw on the ground or in other places, such as lakes and streams.

mold: a hollow shape into which substances are placed while they are still soft from being heated. When heated plastic cools and then hardens inside a mold, it takes on the shape of the mold.

oil: a greasy substance usually found in liquid form that can be used in fuel. Oil deposits in the form of petroleum can often be found in the ground.

pollution: the gas, smoke, trash, and other harmful substances that ruin our environment.

pressure: a strong force applied by one object or body on another.

recycle: to make a new product from an old product that has already been used. Many metal, glass, plastic, and paper products can be recycled.

sterilize: to make an item so clean there are no germs on it. Glass bottles can be sterilized by boiling them in water.

suffocate: to kill a living thing by preventing it from breathing.

thermoplastics: plastics that melt when they are heated. Most plastics we use every day are thermoplastics.

thermosets: plastics that are hard and that do not melt when exposed to heat.

PLACES TO WRITE AND VISIT

Here are some places you can write or visit for more information about plastic and how it can be recycled. If you write, be sure to include your name and address and be clear about the type of information you would like to know. Include a self-addressed, stamped envelope for a reply.

Greenpeace Foundation
185 Spadina Avenue
Sixth Floor
Toronto, Ontario
M5T 2C6

The Exploratorium
  Palace of Arts
  and Sciences
3601 Lyon Street
San Francisco, CA 94123

The National Recycling
  Coalition
1101 30th Street NW
Suite 305
Washington, D.C. 20007

INTERESTING FACTS ABOUT PLASTIC

Did you know . . .

▸ that certain charitable organizations can profit from your recycling? If you give them the recyclable plastic, metal, glass, and paper you have gathered, they can then sell it to recycling plants.

▸ that you can cut down on plastic waste by using metal silverware and glass or ceramic drinking cups?

▸ that doctors have helped people by replacing defective hip and knee joints with plastic ones? Some people have even benefited from receiving plastic hearts!

▸ that plastic containers cannot be used over again like glass bottles because the sterilization process would melt them?

MORE BOOKS TO READ

Earthwise at Home: A Guide to the Care and Feeding of Your Planet.
   Linda Lowery (Carolrhoda)

Garbage and Recycling. Judith Woodburn (Gareth Stevens)

Plastics. Terry Cash (Garrett Educational Corporation)

Plastics. Jacqueline Dineen (Enslow Publishers)

Trash Attack: Garbage and What We Can Do About It.
   Candace Savage (Firefly Books)

Why Does Litter Cause Problems? Isaac Asimov (Gareth Stevens)

INDEX